Glimpses into Life
Through the Bible

5. God of Justice and Just Peace

Glimpses into Life Through the Bible

5. *God of Justice and Just Peace*

Samuel Amirtham & Israel Selvanayagam

ISPCK

2013

Glimpses into Life Through the Bible: *5. God of Justice and Just Peace*—Published by Rev. Dr. Ashish Amos of the Indian Society for Promoting Christian Knowledge (ISPCK), Post Box 1585, 1654 Madarsa Road, Kashmere Gate, Delhi-110006.

ISBN: 978-81-8465-294-9

Laser typeset by **ISPCK,** Post Box 1585,
1654 Madarsa Road, Kashmere Gate, Delhi-110006
Tel: 23866322, 23866323
e-mail–ashish@ispck.org.in • ella@ispck.org.in

website-www.ispck.org.

Contents

Preface to the Series

⇢⊱◈◈◈◐⅜⋘ ⇢⊱◈◈◈◐⅜⋘

We regard this as a privilege to connect with average English speaking Christians. While biblical scholarship is steered to deeper, broader and higher avenues with ever increasing sophistication, Christians in the pews, worshiping Sunday after Sunday, and listening to preacher after preacher, continue to remain in ignorance about the way the Bible has to be approached and its message appropriated. In spite of all our exhortation, pastors seem to have other priorities in ministry than reading the Bible and praying with them. Priests of Jesu-Baal, the growing cult all over the world with different labels, flashing images and manipulative techniques of mass media, appear to be flourishing in terms of five star life-styles and more-star wealth. When challenged, they say that theologians and Bible scholars mislead people with their worldly wisdom and cunning methods. Of course we do not want to continue in the word-game or battle with them. There is clear and frequent warning against false prophets in the Bible. But when trained theologians or pastors and fundamentalist preachers blame one another as false prophets, we have no other option than to leave for God and God's judgment!

This booklet is the fifth of a series of at least 12 booklets we have decided to produce. We, as duos have had previous experience of writing similar booklets but in the language of Tamil. Starting from 1980 and completing 20 booklets in 2003, some of them have undergone several reprints and revisions. Since then they have been classified into two volumes and published with the same title, i.e., *Thirumaraikku Thirumpuvom* (Return to the Word of God, Vol. I in 2008 and Vol. II in 2011) by the Arasaradi Publications of the Tamilnadu Theological Seminary, Madurai. There have been a few asking for the English translation of these booklets. However, we are not in a position to do it and therefore we leave it for others to do.

In a slightly different style and approach, more engaging and detailed, we have come forward to produce these booklets. We the writers are different in age, background, aptitude, experience and perspectives. However, we have a unique kind of blood relation, i.e. bound together by the sacramental blood of Jesus Christ. It is our joy and hope that pastors and congregation members, as individuals and groups, engage with us and with God, reading them and feed-backing to us. In a context of fundamentalist literature littered everywhere that has created a confusing and stumbling jumble, please do not ignore ours even if you reject them after reading! Be assured of our prayerful faith journey with you.

When we approached with the proposal, Dr Ashish Amos, the General Secretary of the ISPCK, responded positively and happily. We are grateful to him and his staff team who have played different roles to get these booklets into your hands. All glory and honour be to our Triune God, the greatest companion in our journey.

Samuel Amirtham & Israel Selvanayagam
Lent 2013

God of Justice
and Just Peace

1.   Welcome!

The word justice is terrifying on the one hand and
consoling on the other. The Bible proclaims that God is just.
He rules the world with justice. That means those involved
in doing injustice cannot go in their way for ever. They will
be brought to justice both in this world and after. On the
other hand God has special favour for those who are victims
of injustice. Their long cry appears to be in vain but at some
point in their life they will be vindicated.

Concern for justice is not confined to religious
enclosures and exhortations. Nor even to law courts. Cry
for justice echoes in political headquarters, administrative

departments, market places, living places and so on. The Bible is full of cries for justice. Those committed to justice join the cries and work in solidarity with the victims of injustice. They find Bible to be a unique book in dealing with this issue. Hence their taking the Bible a weapon of the struggle for justice. But those who favour only the 'beautiful word and wonderful word' might completely miss its voice for justice.

The 10th General Assembly of the World Council of Churches is scheduled to meet from the 30th of October to the 8th of November 2013 in Busan, a Southport city of South Korea. The chosen theme is 'God of Life, Lead us to Justice and Peace.' Preparatory meetings are being organized all over the world. It is a stark reality that in spite of development in all fields all over the world humanity has not solved the issue of persons and communities being crushed by systems of injustice. Some of them are systemic such as the caste system and untouchability in India. Executors of justice often turn to be exploitators of the poor and the weak.

In the backdrop of the above factors we are reflecting on justice and peace. Though the issues of justice and peace concern all thinking people, the Christian community is called to be a witness to the God of justice and engage in issues of justice in the local area. When the disciples were worried about their daily concerns and cores, Jesus said famously: 'But seek first his kingdom and his righteousness, all these things will be given to you as well (Mtt. 6: 33).' They need to be careful in dealing with the issue and avoiding violence in the name of justice and inaction in the name of peace. The phrase 'just peace' should be taken seriously.

2.   Cry for Justice

When Cain murdered his innocent brother Abel the Lord said to Cain: 'What have you done? Listen! Your brother's blood cries out to me from the ground. Now you are under a curse and driven from the ground, which opened its mouth to receive your brother's blood from your hand (Gen. 4: 10f).' Similarly, Hagar, a slave-woman, victimised by family sensibilities, pregnant but standing in a wilderness, named the Lord as the 'God of seeing(16: 13).' She saw that God had seen her plight. The same thing happened when the Hebrew slaves in Egypt 'groaned in their slavery and cried out, and their cry for help because of their slavery went up to God (Ex. 2: 23).' God heard their cry and initiated a process of liberation. These stories represent the cries of victims in all time and all places.

Job cried for justice. In his debate with his friends one question asked was 'Does God pervert justice (Bildad, Job. 8: 3)?' Job asked that if his suffering was a matter of justice who could summon God (9: 19)? Job anguished saying,

'Though I cry "I have been wronged!" I get no response; though I call for help, there is no justice (19: 7). ' Job claimed, 'I put on righteousness as my clothing; justice was my robe and my turban (29: 14). ' Elihu's reasoning and question was: 'It is unthinkable that God would do wrong, that the Almighty would pervert justice... 'Can he who hates justice govern? Will you condemn the just and mighty One (34: 12,17)?' He continued to say, 'now you are laden with the judgment due to the wicked; judgment and justice have taken hold of you (36: 17).' Finally, who was just and righteous and who was wrong? You may initiate a discussion in the youth group or women fellowship in your church.

Not only cries, there are several observations made about justice. Probably most of these affirmations came from victims of injustice. For example, 'To do what is right and just is more acceptable to the Lord than sacrifice... When justice is done, it brings joy to the righteous but terror to evildoers (Prov. 21: 3, 15).' 'Evil men do not understand justice, but those who seek the Lord understand it fully (28: 5).' 'The righteous care about justice for the poor, but the wicked have no such concern (29: 7).' 'And I saw something else under the sun: In the place of judgment wickedness was there (Eccl. 3: 16).' Further, God's judgment is affirmed.

Prophet Isaiah in identification with the victims of Justice makes a public appeal: 'Seek justice, encourage the oppressed. Defend the cause of the fatherless, plead the case of the widow (Is. 1:17).' He observed Jerusalem saying, 'See how the faithful city has become a harlot! She once was full of justice; righteousness used to dwell in her – but now murderers (1: 21)!' He continues to say: 'Your rulers are rebels, companions of thieves; they all love bribes and chase after gifts. They do not defend the cause of the fatherless; the widow's case does not come before them (1: 23). The cry of orphens and widows then reach God. Among his people ' he (God) looked for justice, but saw bloodshed; for righteousness, but heard cries of distress (5: 7).' Jeremiah sends the following message to the royal family about a victim: 'Administer justice every morning; rescue from the hand of his oppressor the one who has been robbed (Jer. 21: 12; 22: 3).' Through Ezekiel the following message was communicated: 'The people of the land practice extortion and commit robbery; they oppress the poor and the needy and mistreat the alien, denying them justice (Eze. 22: 29). A righteous person is the one 'who does not commit robbery but gives his food to the hungry and provides clothing for the naked. He does not lend at usury or take excessive interest. He withholds his hand from doing wrong and judges fairly between man and man (18: 7-8).' Think of the cries for justice of millions today!

3.   God of Justice

There is a key text with this declaration: 'For the Lord is a
God of justice. Blessed are all who wait for him (Is. 30:18).'
All other affirmations and declarations are based on this
cardinal truth. Another expression is 'For I, the Lord, love
justice (61: 8).' Moses sings: 'He is the Rock, his works are
perfect, and all his ways are just. A faithful God who does no
wrong, upright and just is he (Deut. 32: 4).'

Psalmists declare: 'The Lord reigns forever, he has
established his throne of judgment. He will judge the world
in righteousness; he will govern the peoples with justice.
The Lord is a refuge for the oppressed, a stronghold in time
of trouble (Ps. 9: 7-9).' 'The Lord loves righteousness and
justice; the earth is full of his unfailing love (33: 5).' 'He will
make your righteousness shine like the dawn, the justice of
your cause like the noonday sun (37: 6).' 'For the Lord loves
the just and will not forsake his faithful ones...The mouth
of the righteous man utters wisdom, and his tongue speaks
what is just (37: 28-30).' 'I will sing of your love and justice;
to you, O Lord, I will sing praise (101: 1).' A most beautiful
and inspiring stanza of a psalm has captured the imagination
of many: *'Love and faithfulness meet together; righteousness and
peace kiss each other (85: 10).'* 'The Lord works righteousness
and justice for all the oppressed (103: 6).' 'I know that the
Lord secures justice for the poor and upholds the cause of

the needy. Surely the righteous will praise your name and the upright will live before you (140: 12-13; cf. 146: 7).'

The Prophets were also committed to establishing justice for the sake of their God. For example, Isaiah writes: 'The Lord Almighty will be exalted by his justice, and the holy God will show himself holy by his righteousness (Is. 5:16).' The Messiah, the anointed one of God, was supposed to establish justice. 'He will reign on David's throne and over his kingdom, establishing and upholding it with justice and righteousness from that time on and forever (9: 7; see also 16: 5; 28:6, 17; 32: 1; 42: 1ff; 33: 15).' 'Justice will dwell in the desert and righteousness live in the fertile field (32: 16).' God's compassion and graciousness is closely connected with his justice (30: 18).

As justice is foundational of all life and all relationship, those who have gone astray have the only hope is return to God and reorient in a life of justice. Jeremiah, perhaps representing the 'people of God' who had gone astray says: 'Correct me Lord, but only with justice – not in your anger, lest you reduce me to nothing (Jer. 10: 24).' For such correction requires an acknowledgement that God sees everything that happens inside and outside of one's life. One laments with a question: '...to deny a man his rights before the Most High, to deprive a man of justice – would not the Lord see such things (Lam. 3: 35f)?' Prophet Ezekiel gives a profound insight into God's dealing with people. The Lord speaks: 'I will search for the lost and bring back the strays. I will bind up the injured and strengthen the weak, but the sleek and the strong I will destroy. I will shepherd the flock with justice (Eze. 34: 16).' Prophet Hosea stresses this further: 'But you must return to your God; maintain love and justice, and wait for your God always (Hos. 12: 6).'

Amos, an eighth century prophet was thunderous in proclaiming justice or condemning injustice. He attacked those who turned justice into bitterness and cast righteousness to the ground (Am. 5: 7). Similarly, he was heavy on those who turned justice into poison and the fruits of righteousness into bitterness (6: 12). After denouncing meaningless rituals and celebrations he said, '*But let justice roll on like a river, righteousness like a never-failing stream* (5: 24).' This verse has been repeatedly presented in writings and preaching.

It is often reminded that the Israelites were chosen by God so that they would be a witness to all nations. One reminder comes in the following way: 'Listen to me, my people; The law will go out from me, my justice will become a light to the nations (Is. 51: 4). Salvation too is closely connected with Justice and the revelation of God's righteousness (56: 1). Therefore those who do take God seriously, spontaneously do what is right and just.

Few Gentile rulers came to acknowledge Yahweh the God of justice. Here is an example: ' Now I, Nebuchadnezzar, praise and exalt and glorify the King of heaven, because everything he does is right and all his ways are just. And those who walk in pride he is able to humble (Dan. 4: 37).

Thus when we say God loves justice and righteousness but at the same time compassionate and merciful, a stream of reflection spring from it. For example, that means that God cannot be manipulated by acts of ritual sacrifice and devotion. And no one can hide from God. God sees and hears every small bit of details in the life of humans and in the society. Even when proclaim God's compassion and mercy we have to add that they cannot bypass justice. However, when someone feels too pushed to corner and finding a hope the God of justice always provides a way out and this we will point out later. In the mean time we have to observe that any valid creed or faith affirmation must have the cardinal clause that the Lord is God of justice.

4.   Moral Justice

Justice in the area of moral life concerns both individuals and the society. When God created the world and humans he planted a tree of good and evil the fruit of which was forbidden. It symbolized the limit God set for human life. Tempted by the devil Adam and Eve ate the fruit of this tree with a desire to become like God. Instead they became naked and ashamed. The tree of good and evil is planted in human consciousness and social systems. Good relationship with fellow humans, good conduct of keeping the life orderly, careful and healthy sex at appropriate stage in life etc are covered by moral justice.

When moral justice is pushed beyond the limit destruction happens. There is a famous story in the Bible. People of the twin city of Sodom and Gomorrah turned to be so wicked. The Lord said:

> The outcry against Sodom and Gomorrah is so great and their sin so grievous that I will go down and see if what they have done is as bad as the outcry that has reached me. If not, I will know (Gen. 18: 20f).

Earlier, there is a remark on Abraham and his life:

> I have chosen (Abraham), so that he will direct his children and his household after him to keep the way of the Lord by doing what is right and just, so that the Lord will bring about for Abraham what he has promised him (18: 19).

Interestingly, Abraham did not rejoice over his special favour with God but dared to plead with God for averting any destruction of those cities. His starting point was, 'Will you sweep away the righteous with the wicked? What if there are fifty righteous people in the city? Will you really sweep it away and not spare the place for the sake of the fifty righteous people in it? Far be it from you to do such – to kill the righteous with the wicked, treating the righteous and the wicked alike. Far be it from you! Will not the Judge of all the earth do right?'

The Lord replied saying, 'If I find fifty righteous people in the city of Sodom, I will spare the whole place for their sake (18: 23-26).' In the further dialogue the bargain went from fifty down to ten but even that was wanting. Consequently Sodom Gomorrah was destroyed. Abraham's nephew Lot and his family were saved because they were righteous and just. This story was remembered in the early church. For instance, Jude notes, 'Sodom and Gomorrah and the surrounding towns gave themselves up to sexual immorality and perversion. They serve as an example of those who suffer the punishment of eternal fire (Jude 7).'

What do we learn from the above story? Firstly, the foundation of the society and the word is justice. Sexual morality is part of that. However, there are countries, societies and communities where sexual freedom is insisted. Consequently, teenage pregnancies, divorces and children having to live with multiple parents have created untold problems and miseries. Those who are seeped into the system falsely think that it is part of a developed and civilized society. One area in these countries where significant development has been achieved is road traffic. There traffic lights with red, amber and green colours. If they are not there or do not work there will be utter chaos causing fatal accidents. You might wonder that if the same system is applied to sexual morality there could be life with greater satisfaction and fulfillment.

Secondly, even today it is true that because of righteous and just people in desirable good proportion only the world, countries and our society are stable. Otherwise they would certainly collapse. God spoke through Jeremiah: 'Go up and down the streets of Jerusalem, look around and consider, search through her squares. If you can find but one person who deals honestly and seeks the truth, I will forgive this city (Jer. 5: 1).' Subsequently, Jerusalem was destroyed. What about today in our context? Sometimes, it may look like that there is no one righteous in our city or village. Often we look for righteous people within our community, church and the society. We should believe that there are more righteous people in the world than we know. They may be in other religions and secular movements too. For example, Peter in Cornelius' place declared, 'I now realize how true it is that God does not show favouritism but accepts men from every nation who fear him and do what is right (Acts 10: 34-35). As Cornelius was such a person the gospel message was to approve it and lead further.

5.   Political Justice

Power and authority belongs to God. But God is not autocratic but democratic. God devolves power with rulers and governors. They are supposed to devolve it further and makes sure that every individual's right is protected. One of the first injunctions the Israelites received was this: 'Do not follow the crowd in doing wrong. When you give testimony in a lawsuit, do not pervert justice by siding with the crowd, and do not show favouritism to a poor man in his lawsuit (Ex. 23: 2-3; see also v. 6).' Later Moses reminded the community: '*Do not pervert justice or show partiality. Do not accept a bribe, for a bribe blinds the eyes of the wise and twists the words of the righteous. Follow justice and justice alone, so that you may live and possess the land the Lord your God is giving you* (Deut. 16: 19-20).' 'Cursed is the man who withholds justice from the alien, the fatherless or the widow (Deut. 27: 19).'

Even then the history of Israel did not achieve political justice. Samuel was great and honest. 'But his sons did not walk in his ways. They turned aside dishonest gain and accepted bribe and perverted justice (1Sam. 8: 3).' Absalom was cunning enough to steal the hearts of the people by speaking the justice language. He said: 'if only I were appointed judge in the land! Then everyone who has a complaint or case could come to me and I would see that he gets justice…Absalom behaved in this way toward all the Israelites who came to the king asking for justice, so he stole the hearts of the men of Israel (2 Sam. 15: 4-6).' He created a great nuisance to his father David. Of course David himself at times went beyond the limits of his power.

Solomon at the beginning appeared to be justice oriented. His first verdict over a case proved him to be ingenious. 'All Israel heard the verdict the king had given, they held the king in awe, because they saw that he had wisdom from God to administer justice (1 Kgs. 3: 28).' The visiting Queen Sheba attested Solomon's wisdom to maintain justice (10: 9; 2 Chr. 9: 8).' But Solomon's mask is unveiled by a prophetic narration of his life. To start with Solomon had a scandalous birth as his mother was someone else's wife whom his father David murdered in order to take his mother. The first child died. God wanted to move the history on. When Solomon was born God sent the prophet Nathan and gave him a special name Jedidiah meaning 'loved by the Lord (2 Sam. 12: 25).' Solomon proved to be wise in his dealings but later set the record of one of the most wicked kings of history.

When Solomon became the king he annihilated all his potential opponents. He built a palace that took 13 years and a temple that took 7 years. There are different versions about the background of the temple building. Obviously his father David made preparations. He got the timber from

Hiram the king of Tyre and in lieu he gave him 20 barren villages. Thus he cheated Hiram. Solomon levied heavy poll tax and for the first time introduced forced labour in Israel. Read patiently 1 Kgs. Chapters 1-11 for getting the full view of Solomon. God gave a conditional approval of the temple that if Solomon did not follow the path of justice the temple would become a desolate place. Of course that exactly happened. The conclusion of Solomon's life has a most tragic account: his love for foreign wives led him to worship their gods and build shrines. 'He had seven hundred wives of royal birth and three hundred concubines and his wives led him astray... The Lord became angry with Solomon because his heart had turned away, the Lord, the God of Israel, who had appeared to him twice... (1 Kgs. 11: 9ff). Then it is erroneous to take Solomon as a model but a warning. Because of his tyranny after Solomon the kingdom broke into two and this brought many justice issues the people had to face. It was in this context that the Lord God was invoked to rule and prayed to for establishing justice.

It was a prayer-song of people: 'Endow the king with your justice, O God, the royal son with your righteousness. He will judge your people in righteousness, your afflicted ones with justice (Ps. 72: 1-2).' 'Righeousness and justice are the foundation of your throne; love and faithfulness go before you (89: 14; cj. 94: 15; 97: 2).' When many kings went astray forgetting the Lord's injunctions the people proclaimed God as the ideal king. For example:

> The Lord reigns, let the nations tremble; he sits enthroned between the cherubim, let the earth shake. Great is the Lord in Zion; he is exalted over all the nations…The King is mighty, he loves justice-you have established equity; in Jacob you have done what is just and right…(99: 1-3).

Those political leaders who establish justice and activists who fight for justice deserve great appreciation and approval when viewed from the above message.

Who are the blessed? A psalmist answers: 'Blessed are they who maintain justice, who constantly do what is right (106: 3; see also 112: 5).'A wise man observes: 'By justice a king gives a country stability, but one who is greedy for bribes tears it down (Prob. 29: 4).' When this justice fails God is the only refuge for the poor and righteous. 'Many seek an audience with a ruler, but it is from the Lord that man gets justice (29: 26).' Another wise suggests: 'If you see the poor oppressed in a district, and justice and rights denied, do not be surprised at such things, for one official is eyed by a higher one, and over them both are others higher still. The increase from the land is taken by all; the king himself profits from the fields (Eccl. 5: 8- 9).' This picture may be translated into our own context.

In the context of many evil kings, through Jeremiah God gave a testimony to the young king Josiah: '...*He did what was right and just, so all went well with him. He defended the cause of the poor and needy, and so all went well, is that not what it means to know me* (Jer. 22: 15f)?' Through Ezekiel God tells: 'O princes of Israel! Give up your violence and oppression and do what is just and right. Stop dispossessing my people...(Eze. 45: 9).' The way most kings and princes ruled Israel (later Israel and Judah) it came to the light that it was a grave mistake that people had asked Samuel for a king. There could be alternative ways of establishing a political system which could be conducive to justice and righteousness.

6.   Economic Justice

The fundamental affirmation is: 'The earth is the Lord's, and everything in it, the world, and all who live in it; for he founded it upon the seas and established upon the waters (Ps. 24: 1-2).' Once the question of ownership is settled the rest is clear. Out of wrong notion, greed humans grab and exploit with the sole pursuit of 'I and mine.' It has to be replaced by a redeemed consciousness which is captivated by a sense of 'we and ours.' The Bible does not provide an economic theory nor does it provide a system but there are instances and stories which extol equality.

The tendency to grab and accumulate needs to be restrained. We have a telling story in the life of the Father of Faith which we have quoted in no. 3 of this series. After winning a war with the help of 318 trained men in his household, Abraham returned to the king of Sodom with goods, rescued people and his men. The king said to Abraham, 'give me the people and keep the goods for yourself.' You might imagine that some devout person would accept it saying 'Praise the Lord, Hallelujah!' But see what Abraham did. He said to that alien king, 'I have raised my hand to the Lord, God Most High, Creator of heaven and earth, and have taken an oath that I will accept nothing belonging to you, not even a thread or the thong of a sandal, so that you will never be able to say, "I made Abraham rich." I will accept nothing but what my men have eaten and the share belongs to the men who went with me…(Gen. 14: 21-24). Imagine what would have been the response of that king!

During exodus in the wilderness God tested the Israelites if they were content with what was given and observed the commandments (Ex. 16: 4-5). The miraculous and mysterious food manna was given with a principle of equality. Accordingly, 'The Israelites did as they were told; some gathered much, some little. And when they measured it by the omer, he who gathered much did not have too much, and he who gathered little did not have too little. Each one gathered as much as he needed (16: 17-18).' They were supposed to gather twice the measure on the previous day of the Sabbath so that they did not have to go out to gather food on Sabbath. 'Nevertheless, some of the people went out on the seventh day to gather it, but they found none (16: 27). Thus from the beginning the Israelites were taught to consider economic justice as fundamental to their faith.

We do not live in an ideal society but we should take note of experiments prescribed with a view to avoid inequality. The following is what God commanded to the Israelites of whom some would have become poor due to life's exigencies and tragedies:

> Count off seven Sabbaths of years – seven times seven years – so that the seven Sabbaths of years amount to a period of forty-nine years. Then have the trumpet sounded everywhere on the tenth day of the seventh month; on the Day of Atonement sound the trumpet throughout your land. Consecrate the fiftieth year and proclaim liberty throughout the land to all its inhabitants. It shall be a jubilee for you; each one of you is to return to his family property and each to his own clan (Levi. 25: 8-10).

You may ask, why was it not implemented? The reason was establishment of monarchy. There was great shift from the rural and agrarian set up to urbanized and money oriented system.

Even if the re-sharing of land in the jubilee year was not possible there are strong recommendations to help the poor.

It was a great test for the 'people of God' to look after the poor amongst themselves. One arrangement was that in the seventh year the land was to let lie unplowed and unused. 'The poor among your people may get food from it...Do the same with your vineyard and your olive grove (Ex. 23:10f).' More regular arrangement was: 'When you reap the harvest of your land, do not reap to the very edges of your field or gather the gleanings of your harvest. Leave them for the poor and the alien. I am the Lord your God (Levi. 23: 22). There was always concession for the poor in giving offering and other levies (e.g. 14: 21).

In the book of Deuteronomy both the ideal vision and actuality are mentioned. For instance, read chapter 15. Following mention of debt cancellation, v4 says: 'However, there should be no poor among you, for in the land the Lord your God is giving you to possess as your inheritance, he will richly bless you.' V7-8 states: 'If there is a poor man among your brothers in any of the towns of the land...do not be hardhearted or tightfisted towards your poor brother. Rather be openhanded and freely lend him whatever he needs.' The debt cancellation in every seventh year is mentioned as a new lease of life for the poor. V11 points out the possible actuality: 'There will always be poor people in the land. Therefore I command you to be openhanded toward your brothers and toward the poor and needy in your land.'

Recognition of possible actuality should not be taken as a justification for allowing or making the poor to struggle for their survival. Let us never forget the vision in verse 4 that 'there should be no poor among you.'

We have already noted king Solomon and his atrocities. Another example is the story of Naboth's Vineyard. King Ahab asked for the poor man's vineyard which was close to his palace. He asked for it to make a vegetable garden in lieu for which he would give another vineyard or money. Naboth replied, 'The Lord forbid that I should give you the inheritance of my fathers.' As it was unlawful in Israel to take one's inheritance, Ahab went home, sullen and angry, and lay on his bed sulking and refused to eat. His foreign wife could not have sympathy with the system in Israel. Therefore she asked her husband, 'Is this how you act as king over Israel? Get up and eat! Cheer up. I will get you the vineyard of Naboth.' She arranged to murder Naboth and grabbed his land. Then it was history, a bloody history (1 Kgs. 21).

Prophet Amos was a great champion for the cause of the poor. He challenged the rich by saying, 'You trample on the poor and force him to give you grain (Am. 5:11).' One can write an extensive commentary applying the message to international trade practices such as receiving food items in exchange for weapons. We will elaborate it later. How poverty leads to horrible malpractices is the matter we are concerned with here. Amos poined out that 'They sell the righteous for silver, and the needy for a pair of sandals. They trample on the heads of the poor as upon the dust of the ground and deny justice to the oppressed (2: 6f; also read 8: 6).'

In the context of rampant economic injustice Jesus declared that the reign of God belonged to the poor (Lk. 6: 20). Jesus accepted the invitation from few rich for dinner but irritated them by talking about the poor (read ch. 14). He connected economic sharing with salvation. For example, when he visited Zacchaeus he declared that 'Here and now I give half of my possessions to the poor, and if I have cheated anybody out of anything, I will pay back four times the amount.' Immediately Jesus said, 'Today salvation has come to the house (19: 8-10).' Have you ever thought that salvation has to do with economic justice as well. Have you heard any personal testimonies of this type?

There were few individuals to talk about justice for the poor. For example in Prov. 14: 31 we read: 'He who oppresses the poor shows contempt for their Maker, but whoever is kind to the needy honours God.' In 29: 7 we read, 'The righteous care about justice for the poor, but the wicked have no such concern.' You may be inspired to find such proverbs in your vernacular.

Jesus was never allowed to establish economic justice for all. However, his movement which developed into church always remembered the poor. When Paul was commissioned to evangelize the Gentiles there was only one condition. 'All they asked was that we should continue to remember the poor, the very thing I was eager to do (Gal. 2: 10).' Paul collected ('robbed') money from the Gentile churches for the poor Christians in Jerusalem. While writing about this he refers to Ps. 112: 19 which says: 'He has scattered abroad his gifts to the poor; his righteousness endures for ever (1 Cori. 9: 9). He recalls the principle of equality too:

> Our desire is not that others might be relieved while you are hard pressed, but that there might be equality. At the present time your plenty will supply what they need, so that in turn their plenty will supply what you need. Then there will be equality, as it is written: 'He who gathered much did not have too much, and he who gathered little did not have too little (2 Cori. 8: 13-15; cf. Ex. 16: 18).'

This concern continued. Apostle James ridicules the rich and their possessions and those ill treat the poor (Js. 5: 1-7). If read carefully one can find in the Book of Revelation challenging insights into the unjust economic system and operation of the Imperial Rome against which the Jews and Christians fought. If there is a living church this fight will continue.

7. Judicial Justice

One of the injunctions received by Moses is as follows:

> Do not follow the crowd in doing wrong. When you give testimony in a lawsuit, do not pervert justice by siding with the crowd, and do not show favouritism to a poor man in his lawsuit.
>
> Do not deny justice to your poor people in their lawsuits. Have nothing to do with a false charge and do not put an innocent or honest person to death, for I will not acquit the guilty (Ex. 23: 3, 6).
>
> Do not pervert justice; do not show partiality to the poor or favouritism to the great, but judge your neighbor fairly (Lev. 19: 15).

You will agree with us that these injunctions need to be written not only in the court rooms but also in conscience of all the judges, advocates and witnesses.

From the time of liberation to near-settlement Moses was judging the cases of people. When it came to be too much he was asked to share the spirit and responsibility with seventy leaders. Moses reluctantly accepted. When the Israelites settled in Canaan their cases and disputes were settled by Judges who also were rulers and army chiefs. This tradition ended with Samuel. The sense of justice of that time is remarkably evident in Samuel's farewell speech. He said:

> I am old and gray, and my sons are here with you. I have been your leader from my youth to until this day. Here I stand. Testify against

me in the presence of the Lord and his anointed. Whose ox have I taken? Whose donkey have I taken? Whom have I cheated? Whom have I oppressed? From whose hand have accepted a bribe to make me shut my eyes? If I have done any of these, I will make it right (1 Sam. 12: 2-3).

The people replied in the negative. Then came kingship and we have already seen aspects of political justice. Here we will point out the key verses on judicial justice.

'A wicked man accepts a bribe in secret to pervert the course of justice (Prov. 17: 23).' 'It is not good to be partial to the wicked or to deprive the innocent of justice (18: 5).' 'A corrupt witness mocks at justice, and the mouth of the wicked gulps down evil (19: 28).' The Ecclesiast observes: 'In the place of judgment-wickedness was there, in the place of justice-wickedness was there (Eccl. 3:16).' Prophet Isaiah was more categorical and pointed:

Woe to those who make unjust laws, to those who issue oppressive decrees, to deprive the poor of their rights and withhold justice from the oppressed of my people, making widows their pray and robbing the fatherless (Is. 10: 1-2).

In the same vein Amos tells the house of Israel that 'You oppress the righteous and take bribes and you deprive the poor of justice in the courts (Am. 5: 12). We remember John the Baptist and Jesus who were victims of political manipulation and partial judgment.

Imagine Isaiah, Amos, John and Jesus visiting our courts! Every court room has the caption written on the wall: 'Truth will win.' Do you think that truth wins in every judgment? Our goddess of justice stands as a statue blind-folded. Can she see and understand the position of the poor? We are repeatedly told that the Indian judiciary is corrupt and procrastination of cases breed corruption in unimaginable proportions! Who will adopt court campuses as our mission field?

8.   Trade Justice

It is a question if market and morality go together. The ancient practice of barter system, that is exchange of goods, there was greater transparency and fairness than the monetary system that came later. *Market rules the world and our life as it is observed*. The Bible is concerned about the trade justice which may be shocking for those who are engaged in business.

When Abraham was among the Hittites his wife Sara died. Abraham needed a burial cave. The Hittites, out of their great respect for Abraham, asked him to take the choicest cave and no one would refuse. But Abraham insisted payment. He said: 'If you are willing to bury my dead, then listen to me and intercede with Ephron son of Zohar on my behalf so that he will sell me the cave of Machpelah, which belongs to him and is at the end of this field. Ask him to sell it to me

for the full price as a burial site among you (Gen. 23: 8-9)).'
Ephron pleaded him not to make a big deal. But Abraham
persisted on payment. Finally, 'Abraham agreed to Ephron's
terms and weighed out for him the price he had named in
the hearing of the Hittites: four hundred shekels of silver,
according to the weight current among the merchants (23:
16).' When such an openness and transparency is practiced
there is no room for manipulation and corruption.

There was a commandment against dishonest scales and
measures: 'Do not use dishonest standards when measuring
length, weight or quantity. Use honest scales and honest
weights, an honest ephah, and an honest hin (Lev. 19: 35f).

A wise person declares: 'The Lord detests differing
weights, and dishonest scales do not please him (Prov. 20:
23; also 11: 1).' 'Honest scales and balances are from the
Lord; all the weights in the bag are of his making (16: 11).
Hosea after observing the practice in a market place speaks
God's word saying 'The merchant uses dishonest scales; he
loves to defraud (Hos. 12: 7).' In the same context Micah
speaks: 'Shall I acquit a man with dishonest scales, with a bag
of false weights? (Mic. 6: 11)' In Ezekiel's vision for a new
city, he is asked to use accurate scales etc (Eze. 45:10). He
also says: 'You are to use accurate scales, an accurate ephah
and an accurate bath. The ephah and the bath are to be the
same size, the bath containing a tenth of a homer; the homer

is to be the standard measure for both. The shekel is to consist of twenty gerahs. Twenty shekels plus twenty-five shekels plus fifteen shekels equal one mina (45: 10). Modern system of scales, weights etc may differ but the spirit behind the injunctions is the same. Do you see inaccurate scales used in sales?

You may say that we have now electronic weighing machines. Mind, it is not infallible. Only experts will explain you the possibility of maladjustments. Another tactic followed in shops is that you are asked to pay the maximum retail price. Have you ever asked about the minimum and the middle price? If there are tax differences in different states the accurate price could be printed noting different prices in different states!

When we say that market rules our life one aspect of it is that we are forced to pay for what we may view it as nonsense. You have flashing advertisements on the TV screen and blasted through radio. Some may be amusing but most are fooling us. Our phone contact is intervened by sales advertisement. Internet services thrives on disturbing us with flashing advertisements. To add to the credit of the advertisements cine stars and sports stars are used to appear on the TV screen recommending the particular products. Our culture has gone to a detestable stage that these stars are the authenticating authorities of what we use and what we have to eat. We are also tempted to ask whether those stars sell their self-dignity for money. And it is glaring that while the sports grounds are adorned with adverts of multinational corporations, the sports starts' dress, from socks to hats, carry the emblems and words of different business establishments. You may pity on them because they are not allowed to stand for what they are but what they are not.

On 11 September 2001 the twin towers of the World Trade Centre in New York were dramatically knocked down by aero planes which had been hijacked. About three thousand people died and several injured. The whole world was shocked. Different interpretations of this hoary event have been given. But the most acceptable one has been that it was the collective anger expressed against the domination of the developed countries on behalf of the victims. Around that time and even after there have been cases of mass suicide of farmers in India because they were forced to buy seeds and cultivate with prescribed specifications that overwhelmed them. Due to unjust trade policies children in poor countries were dying on the streets.

Many Non-governmental organizations have been asking for a just and fair dealing of trade which will have the principle of transparency. When people say that business is more lucrative than other professions we need to ask questions about market and morality. The allowance behind 'buy one get one free' does not show the generosity of the seller but their manipulative and exploitative technique.

9.   Eco Justice

Today one of the most alarming concerns is the health and balance of the environment. Thoughtless over-exploitation of the natural resources have caused drought, flood and erratic seasons. Human greed expressed in undue indulgence in consumer goods deprives masses from enjoying the basic needs of life. As we noted above, unregulated market forces with the help of manipulative media push those who can afford to accumulate more without any concern for the poor. We see diet-related obesity on the one hand and emaciated bodies due to malnutrition on the other thus betraying contradiction in life. Thankfully, there is increasing awareness about ecological issues but very often a comprehensive action plan is lacking.

When God created the world he told the humans that, 'Be fruitful and increase in number; fill the earth and subdue it. Rule over the fish of the sea and the birds of the air and over every living creature that moves on the ground (Gen.1: 22).' The text continues to speak about other natural resources for human living. The meaning of the word 'rule' here draws our attention. There have been several exegetical studies that point out that it does not mean domination but service. To support this conclusion a fact from the second creation account is pointed out: 'The Lord God took the man and put him in the Garden of Eden to work it and take care of it (2: 15).' It is the responsibility of the humans to look after the natural world and enjoy its fruits sparingly. They are the vicegerent of the earth and accountable to the creator.

It is dangerous to see the world as human-centred. According to the Scriptures humans are part of the creation, not the centre of it. Even when the flood destroyed the earth Noah and family were not the only ones to go into the saving ark. 'Pairs of clean and unclean animals, of birds and of all creatures that move along the ground, male and female, came to Noah and entered the ark, as God had commanded Noah (Gen. 7: 9).' The description is more picturesque in 7:13-16:

> On that very day Noah and his sons, Shem, Ham and Japheth, together with his wife and the wives of his three sons, entered the ark. They had with them every wild animal according to its kind, all livestock according to their kinds, every creature that moves along the ground according to its kind, everything with wings. Pairs of all creatures that have the breath of life in them came to Noah and entered the ark. The animals going in were male and female of every living thing, as God had commanded Noah. Then the Lord shut him in.

When the flood was over all these people and creatures came out (8: 15-19). The original blessing of 'ruling over' the creatures is repeated in 9: 1-3. The climax of the story is God's covenant with Noah and all the above mentioned creatures as well as for all generations to come. A rainbow was set to mark and seal this covenant (9: 8-17). If this is clear enough how did the idea of human souls being saved by entering into the church, the so called ark of salvation? Such distortion is not the only one in the Christian history.

While the universal covenant that God made through Noah remains valid, there was the particular covenant made with the people of Israel had a special significance. They were expected to realize the universal covenant by concretizing it in their history. Concern for the flora and fauna was central. For example, when God made special provision of the seventh year in which no cultivation of the land was allowed the fruits had to be left for the poor and wild animals (Ex. 23: 10). However, this was forgotten when wicked kings became warmongering, urbanizing and exploiting.

It was left to poets and prophets to keep up a vision for the future. A psalmist tells God, 'When I consider your heavens, the work of your fingers, the moon and the stars, which you have set in place, what is man that you are mindful of him? You made him a little over than the heavenly beings and crowned him with glory and honour (Ps. 8: 3-5; cf. 19:1ff).' The following verses repeat the original blessing of 'ruling over.' We require imagination to deal with the nature and all in it with a sense of awe, wonder and humility.

We hardly include nature in our liturgies of adoration, praise, confession and thanksgiving. Psalm 104 is a great example nature-focused liturgy. It starts with the verse, 'Praise the Lord O my soul. O Lord my God, you are very great; you are clothed with splendor and majesty..' It continues to mention light as God's garment, laying beams of his upper chambers on waters, clouds as his chariot riding on the wings of wind, winds his messengers, flame of fire as his servants; he makes spring pour water into the ravines which gives water to all the beasts of the field; the birds of the air nest by the waters and they sing among the branches; he makes grass grow for the cattle, and plants for humans to cultivate that results in food and drink; the trees of the Lord are well watered, the cedars of Lebanon that he planted; the high mountains belong to the wild goats; the crags are a refuge for the coneys; the sun and moon mark off the seasons, day and night, work and rest; the sea is vast and spacious, teeming with creatures beyond number; God feeds all of them and sustains the life of the planet. Reaffirming praise and confession the poet concludes his song with the words, 'may sinners vanish from the earth and the wicked be no more. Praise the Lord. Songs with such poetic imagination are found more in the secular arena than in the church!

After decrying injustice and desolation prophet Isaiah expresses the joy of the redeemed in ch. 35. 'The desert and the parched land will be glad; the wilderness will rejoice and blossom; it will rejoice greatly and shout for joy. The glory of Lebanon will be given to it, the splendor of Carmel and Sharon; they will see the glory of the Lord, the splendor of our God...Water will gush forth in the wilderness and streams in the desert. The burning sand will become a pool, the thirsty ground bubbling springs. In the haunts where jackals once lay, grass and reeds and papyrus will grow (v1 – 7).'

While anguishing the devastating effects of skillful war, prophet Jeremiah laments: 'I looked at the earth, and it was formless and empty; and at the heavens, and their light was gone. I looked at the mountains, and they were quaking; all the hills were swaying. I looked, and there were no people; every bird in the sky had flown away. I looked, and fruitful land was a desert...'(jer. 4: 23-26). In assessing the effects of war we normally hear how many people were killed and how many injured, but not how much damaged and inflicted in the nature and her resources.

You may ask the question, while we have such a wonderful vision of the nature which is part of salvation, why Christianity talked about more if not only the salvation of the soul? The short answer is that it was due to Hellenistic influence. The long answer is worth pursuing though we do not have place here. However, there are hints where the Hebrew holistic vision was maintained. Apostle Paul, for example, in the context discussing the future hope for the redeemed humans notes: 'We know that the whole creation has been groaning as in the pains of childbirth right up to the present time (Ro. 8: 22).' This is tied with the salvations with their souls as well as bodies. It is very significant to note that the biblical vision for the future includes a city in which will flow a river of the water of life, as clear as crystal. 'On each side of the river stood the tree of life, bearing twelve crops of fruit, yielding its fruit every month. And the leaves of the tree are for the healing of the nations (Rev. 22: 1-2). Without such natural beauty and resources heavenly life will be most boring!

Eco justice is the opposite of ego justice. Those who have realized this have committed to a simple life style; give solidarity to those who protest against dams, deforestation and establishment of nuclear plants and so on. They protest against the use of plastic and thermacole. They raise voice for reducing vehicles. But in spite of that these productions with new models and labels seem to be on the increase. There is no doubt that, as many scientists warn, we will forcibly hit a wall that will be tragic. It requires common sense to realize that our natural resources including crude oil are not unlimited!

10.   Just Peace

A sworn agreement or treaty between two parties was believed to lead to peace between them (Gen. 26: 29). There could be a pact of convenience. The treaty between innocent Laban and cunning Jacob was of this type (31: 45: 55). Jacob had to go through a mysterious experience of transformation that led to limp and make just peace with his brother Esau, Jacob's earliest victim. It involved a reparation which was given in the form of a gift.

Psalmists extol the companionship between justice and peace. The following verse is both poetic and insightful:

> Love and faithfulness meet together; righteousness and peace kiss each other. Faithfulness springs forth from the earth, and righteousness looks down from heaven. The Lord will indeed give what is good and our land will yield its harvest. Righteousness goes before him and prepares the way for his steps (Ps. 85: 10-13).

There are a few verses that stress hope for the future. This is because God's love and compassion is unfailing. Isaiah says that God will fill Zion with justice and righteousness (Is. 33: 5; this is in contrast to the disappointing message of 5: 7). This kind of comity and harmony is presented with slightly different imagination in Is. 11: 1ff. As a consequence of God's judgment with justice and compassion, and the coming of the anointed (Messiah) who has righteousness as his belt and faithfulness as sash around his waist and will establish a peaceable kin-dom in the world. The imagination has a stunning beauty:

> The wolf will live with the lamb, the leopard will lie down with the goat, the calf and the lion and the yearling together; and a little child will lead them. The cow will feed with the bear, their young will lie down together, and the lion will eat straw like the ox. The infant will play near the hole of the cobra, and the young child put his hand into the viper's nest. They will neither harm nor destroy on all my holy mountain, for the earth will be full of the knowledge of the Lord as the waters cover the sea (11: 6-9).

This vision was communicated in the eighth century BCE by Isaiah. In the same century, Micah too communicated a vision. Accordingly, all people will dwell in their places without having to be alarmed and the war weapons will be converted into agricultural tools (Mic. 4: 3-4). Basically it is not peace of mind as proclaimed by fundamentalist preachers, banks and insurance companies. It is a just peace that covers politics, environmental integrity and harmony among people irrespective of religious persuasions.

Jeremiah perceived false peace proclaimed by false priests and prophets. He says: 'From the least to the greatest, all are greedy for gain; prophets and priests alike, all practice deceit. They dress the wound of my people as though it were not serious. "Peace, peace, peace," they say when there is no peace (Jer. 6: 13-14).' He continues to note that such people have no sense of shame. You may rightly think there are so many such preachers and priests around us.

Jesus was born as the prince of peace. The Beatitudes include 'Blessed are those who hunger and thirst for righteousness' and 'Blessed are the peacemakers, for they will be called sons of God (Mtt. 5: 6, 9). You might think that Jesus was always a pacifist and soft-spoken person. As if being aware of Jeremiah's teaching, he said that he did not come to bring peace to the earth but a sword (of justice) that would make division within a family (10: 34-36; cf. Lk. 12: 51). His cleansing of the temple and questioning the one who slapped him show his commitment to justice and at the same time he was committed to peace as well. This does not mean engaging in violence in all cases that appeared to require justice. Jesus lived in a community which was ruled by Rome and there was a strong movement to fight it. Jesus was sharing their concern of liberation, but taking lesson from the history, he pleaded for a peaceful approach (19: 41ff). You may think of situations where deciding between justice and peace is not easy. Needed is collective decision with prayer.

11.   A Chance for New Beginning

One of Archbishop Desmund Tutu's award winning books is titled *No Future without Forgiveness*. When people carry a heavy load of guilt accumulated by wrong doings of unjust nature, what is the way out? The process starts with an affirmation of God as the just and righteous one and compassionate towards those who are repentant. In Isaiah 1: 27 we read, 'Zion will be redeemed with justice, her penitent ones with righteousness.' (see also 33: 5). After a sort of divorce God offers a new betrothal and marriage. Thus he says, 'I will betroth you to me for ever. I will betroth you in righteousness and justice, in love and compassion. I will betroth you in faithfulness, and you will acknowledge the Lord (Hos. 2: 19-20).'

Ezra, in the context of rebuilding Jerusalem after the exile and return of Jews prays to God:

> O Lord God of Israel, you are righteous! We are left this day as a remnant. Here we are before you in our guilt, though because of it not one of us can stand in your presence (Ez. 9: 15).

There is an integral connection between justice and peace: 'The fruit of righteousness will be quietness and confidence for ever. My people will live in peaceful dwelling places, in secure homes, in undisturbed places of rest (Is. 32: 17-18).' There is not a short-cut or crooked way. The repentance should be genuine. God says, 'But if a wicked man turns away from all the sins he has committed and keeps all my decrees and does what is just and right, he will surely live (Eze. 18: 21, 27). There could be the opposite also (18: 25;

cf. 33: 14-16). There is no question about God's dealing in just ways (18: 29).

Justification by faith is one of the central messages of the New Testament. It is not as clear as you think, hence several interpretations. The context was the Jewish community claiming that they pleased God by doing justice which means following the complex system of law, for the same reason they did not accept the Gentiles until they went through the Jewish system. Paul argued that just as Abraham trusted God and was justified the Gentiles were justified by believing Jesus (Rom. 3: 26; 4: 6; Gal. 3: 6). He emphasized the fact that God reconciled the whole world through Christ and the response of humans was to accept that out of divine grace they were accepted though unacceptable (1 Cor. 6: 19). One misunderstanding was to commit sin that grace might abound. Paul corrects this and emphasizes on a life, holy, righteous and peaceful (Rom. 6). When the misunderstanding persisted Apostle James had to stress the importance of faith as well as just action. Paul too came to stress God's justice (2 The. 1: 6). It is dangerous to take advantage of God's mercy and forgiveness and return to injustice again and again. 'It is a dreadful thing to fall into the hands of the living God (Heb. 10: 31).'

www.ingramcontent.com/pod-product-compliance
Lightning Source LLC
LaVergne TN
LVHW041209080426
835508LV00008B/874